EASTER
Program Builder
No. 22

Plays—Skits—Songs
Recitations—Exercises

Compiled by
Paul M. Miller

Lillenas Publishing Co.
Kansas City, MO 64141

An Easter Welcome

We're glad you came
To church today
To hear us sing
And help us pray.

—*Margaret Primrose*

Have a Blessed Easter

May Jesus touch you in a special way,
On this blessed Easter Day.

—*Evangeline Carey*

Happy Easter to You

God truly cares about you,
That's why Jesus lives today.
May the news make your Easter
The best in every way!

—*Evangeline Carey*

Happy Easter

Happy Easter to each of you.
God's giving us a good day too.

—*Margaret Primrose*

Come

When I heard the bells today,
I could almost hear them say:
"Come, come, it is time to sing;
Time to praise the risen King."

—*Margaret Primrose*

The Tomb Is Empty

The tomb is empty,
And Jesus is alive.
May you share the victory!

—*Evangeline Carey*

We Know

(An exercise for three groups of children speaking in unison)

Age Three:
We know we are three.
We know Jesus set us free.

Age Four:
We know we are four.
We know our sins Christ bore.

Age Five:
We know we are five.
We know Jesus is alive!

—*Anna L. Williams*

Christ Rose

Christ rose from the dead.
He has risen just as He said.

—*Anna L. Williams*

A Message of Cheer

I have a message
A message of cheer.
Christ Jesus arose!
Glad Easter is here!

—*Dorothy Conant Stroud*

Just to Say

I stopped by
Just to say
Jesus is alive.
Happy Easter Day!

—*Robert Colbert*

Happy, Happy Easter

In this Easter season,
God seeks from above,
To grant us peace
And His eternal love.

—*Evangeline Carey*

I Hold This Lily

(For a child holding a white lily)

I hold this lily up to say
I wish you happy Easter Day.

—*Vida Munden Nixon*

A Child Speaks

Christ died all to save.
Christ rose from the grave.
Because He lives, I'm here to say
Have a blessed Easter Day!

—*C. R. Sheidies*

The Joy of Easter

May the joy of our risen Lord
Bless your heart and mind
And make your Easter
The best that you can find!

—*Evangeline Carey*

Christ Blessed

I have something
Good to say;
Praise God for this
Christ-blessed Easter Day!

—*Robert Colbert*

Christ Is King

Bright flowers bloom,
And birdies sing
This message sweet,
"Our Christ is King!"

—*Dorothy Conant Stroud*

Easter Is Every Day

We have hope for tomorrow
And strength along the way
Because Jesus is alive,
And Easter is every day!

—*Evangeline Carey*

3

Welcome

Child 1: We are here because
   We have a special part;
   Our greetings come to you
   Right from each heart.

Child 2: Every one of us want you
   To feel real happy here;
   We hope you'll come to our church
   Each week throughout the year.

Child 3: Love is always present
   In everything we do;
   We are mighty glad today
   To see each one of you.

Child 4: Care for family and for friends
   Is important so you see
   That's the kind of church
   We always try to be.

Child 5: Only Jesus is our Guide
   He is our Teacher too.
   We pray to Him each day.
   We'll pray for each of you.

Child 6: Many times we get together
   We have lots of fun;
   If you need a church home
   We invite you to come.

Child 7: Each of us has a card.

(Present letters here.)

Child 7: Now read from left to right:
   See, it says "W E L C O M E."

All: "WELCOME" we say with all our might.

   —*Helen Kitchell Evans*

We're Glad You Came

My shoe has come untied;
   My hair is messed up too,
No matter how I tried
   To do what I should do.

But I did not forget
   The lines I learned to say:
"We're glad you came to church
   This happy Easter Day."

   —*Margaret Primrose*

Welcome . . . Welcome . . . Welcome

Mama bought these clothes for me
   And said to keep them nice.
Mama says to welcome you
   And say it once or twice.
Welcome . . .Welcome . . .Welcome
   Oh well, *three* times is awful nice.

   —*Paul Medford*

An Easter Thank-you

Thanks for Easter lilies,
   For the church bell's happy ding,
Thanks for organ music
   And joyful songs to sing.

Thanks that Jesus loved us
   And for the blood He shed.
But thanks, Lord, most of all,
   That He's no longer dead.

   —*Margaret Primrose*

4

Praise God

Child 1: Praise God for this happy
time!

Child 2: Praise God for His love
sublime!

Child 3: Praise Him in your special
way,
On this happy Easter Day.

Child 4: Bow your head and quietly
pray;
Ask that He take your sins
away.

Child 1: Ask the Christ to enter in
And free your life from fear
and sin.

Child 2: Give you joy instead of sor-
row,
Help you in each new to-
morrow.

Child 3: Ask Him to bless you and
me
And give us life in eternity.

Child 4: Let your heart with glad-
ness chime
At this happy Easter time.

—*Helen Kitchell Evans*

My Prayer of Thanks

The blue and yellow butterfly,
The eagle in her nest up high
Bespeak of God's unfailing love
For each creature beneath His sky.
As God cares for His creation,
So His care for us is sure.
For by His love He came to earth
Our freedom to secure.
On this Easter morning,
I pause, a prayer to say,
To thank Jesus for rising
To bring new life today.
May God bless you this Easter!

—*C. R. Scheidies*

He Is Not Here

(An Easter recitation for four children)

Boy 1: Short pants, long pants, ties,
and shirts;
Eggs and candy and super
desserts.

Girl 1: Ducks and bunnies and
chicks and stuff;
Are fun and pretty, but are
not enough.

Boy 2: Easter morning at break of
day
Jesus rose to show us the
way.

Girl 2: "He is not here," the angel
cried.
He once was dead, but is
now alive.

—*Paul Medford*

Hallelujah!

Easter eggs; Easter lily;
Easter dresses, soft and frilly;
Easter bunnies; Easter hat;
Easter this and Easter that.

What a sing-song little rhyme
With words like drummers marking
time!
With just one word I'd rather say,
Thank the Lord He lives today!
Hallelujah!

—*Margaret Primrose*

Time to Give Thanks

This isn't just a program
Nor just a time to sing.
It's more than just a Sunday
That comes in early spring.

It's Easter and it's time to say:
"We thank You once again
Because You gave Your life for us.
Now bless us all. Amen."

—*Margaret Primrose*

Easter Is the Time

Child 1: Easter is a time for hope.

Child 2: The flowers peep from the
earth;
Easter is the time we see
All nature in rebirth.

Child 1: Easter is a time for joy,

Child 2: When we send cards that
say,
"You are loved throughout
the year
But especially on this Easter Day."

Child 1: Easter is a time for faith,

Child 2: Faith that someday we will
have peace
And see the day when all
wars cease.

Child 1: Easter is a time for praise,

Child 2: Praise for our Father up
above;
A time to let Him know
We are grateful for His
love.

—*Helen Kitchell Evans*

What Easter Means to Me

I like to color Easter eggs
And hunt them in new grass,
Then sit awhile and taste them
While parades of spring clouds
pass.

But in my curls and ruffles,
Just sitting in the pew
And thinking hard of bunnies
Is not enough to do.

For Jesus died and lives again
I want to stand and sing,
"Hallelujah! He arose,
And Jesus is our King."

—*Margaret Primrose*

Triumph

They borrowed a manger
For His bed.
They borrowed some straw
To pillow His head.
Nothing was His own.

He borrowed a lunch
And made it reach.
He borrowed a boat
From which to preach.
Nothing was His own.

But the crown He wears
And the glory He shares
As He sits upon the throne,
And the praises they sing
As they hail Him king,
Those are His very own!

—*Marita M. Root*

He's Alive

The tomb in the rock was sealed
And guarded by brawny men
Who knew the words of Jesus,
"I'll die, but I'll rise again."

The earth quaked; the tomb opened,
And all the guards fled;
For wonder of wonders,
Jesus rose from the dead.

—*Margaret Primrose*

Jesus and Me

Jesus came to earth like me,
To live and grow, to laugh and cry.
But my Jesus never sinned so that
He for my sin might die.

My Jesus died on Calvary
To offer us a whole new way.
But He's not dead today,
He LIVES that you and I
Might ever be set FREE!

—*C. R. Scheidies*

6

What Is Easter?

Is it green-dyed baby chickens
    And chocolate Easter bunnies?
Is it having spring vacation
    And time to watch the funnies?

Is it ham for Sunday dinner
    And hiding colored eggs?
Sweet-smelling Easter lilies,
    Or colts with wobbly legs?

Is it going to church on Sunday
    In your new spring dress and hat
And hoping someone notices?
    Or is it more than that?

Is it a happy celebration
    Of the day an empty tomb
Proved to us the power of God
    And sent Satan to his doom?

—Marita M. Root

Why?

The world is asking:

Almighty God?
    Then tell me why
    He died upon a cross.
Prince of Peace?
    Then why the wars
    Fought at such great cost?
Bread of Life?
    When children starve
    For lack of bread?
Light of the World?
    When darkness reigns
    And fills the world with dread?
King of Kings?
    When wicked men
    Oppress their people so?
Righteous Judge?
    When good men die
    And the guilty are let go?

Because He knew we'd ask, He left us:

The empty tomb
    To prove His power
    To conquer sin and death.

The Holy Spirit
    To comfort us
    And guide our every breath.
His saving grace
    As a reward
    For trusting in His name.
And the Word of God
    To help us know
    The reason that He came.

And He left us these promises:

To come again
    And right the wrongs
    And wipe away our tears.

To reign forever
    To reward the good
    And drive away our fears!

—Marita M. Root

New Life

The birds are coming back again,
    The sun is warm and bright.
Dad helped me find my roller skates
    And fly my brand-new kite.

The crocuses are all in bloom
    Around the willows tall.
The squirrels are digging up the
    nuts
    They buried in the fall.

Don't need my snow boots anymore
    And sometimes not my coat,
But Mother thinks I might catch
    cold
    Or get a bad sore throat.

The farmer's sheep all have lambs
    And hens have baby chicks.
Robins are building nice new nests
    Of bits of string and sticks.

Isn't this a perfect time
    To celebrate the day
Our Savior came to life again
    Before He went away?

—Marita M. Root

He Supplies Our Needs

Chorus: Christ supplies our every
need!
Christ, our Lord, is risen
indeed!

Child 1: Day of gladness, day of
mirth,

Child 2: Joyful time upon the earth;

Child 3: Welcome to the blooming
spring!

Child 4: Let all voices loudly ring!

Chorus: Christ supplies our every
need!
Christ, our Lord, is risen
indeed!

Child 5: King of men, of every na-
tion,

Child 6: Gives to all His great salvation!

Child 7: Jesus shows His true concern

Child 8: From our Bible this we
learn.

Chorus: Christ supplies our every
need!
Christ, our Lord, is risen
indeed!

—*Helen Kitchell Evans*

We Like Easter Sunday

A Playlet for Easter

by Helen Kitchell Evans

Time: A week before Easter

Place: A local church

Cast:
> TOM
> BILL
> SALLY
> JANE
> MRS. WRIGHT

(Each child speaks in the same order, so it's easy for small children to memorize and present.)

TOM: Who likes Easter Sunday?

BILL: I do!

SALLY: I do!

JANE: Me too!

TOM: Why do you like Easter, Bill?

BILL: I like to sing songs!

SALLY: I like to see all the people!

JANE: Me too!

TOM: Do you think we will have our church full of people next Sunday?

BILL: We can if all of us try to get people to come.

SALLY: I'll try to help. I'll call all of my relatives and friends.

JANE: Me too! Me too!

TOM: We have a song to practice, so we better get with it.

9

BILL: Didn't Mrs. Wright say she would be here before long?

SALLY: Here she comes now.

(Enter teacher and any number of singers.)

MRS. WRIGHT: Everyone in place now for our practice. Remember, this is our last time, so do well.

(They sing whatever has been selected and then return to assigned places.)

Ever-Present Friend

Choral for two individuals or groups

by C. R. Scheidies

Staging: Groups on opposite sides of platform/stage

GROUP 1: The rugged cross is empty,

GROUP 2: The grave thrown open wide.

GROUP 1: Come see the place our Savior lay
And where He bled and died.

GROUP 2: For, you see, He is no longer there.

GROUP 1: He has risen as He said,
Victorious over sin and hell . . .

GROUP 2: For He's no longer DEAD!

GROUP 1: Stronger than death and sin and hell,

GROUP 2: He's here today for you and me.

GROUP 1: Strong enough to take our heavy loads

ALL: And set us wholly free!

GROUP 1: So this Easter we thank our Lord,
Who died and rose again,

GROUP 2: For He gave us more than life . . .

ALL: He's our ever-present friend!

Two Temple Guards

by Cynthia S. Baker

A reading play, with parts rehearsed and well read, but not memorized.

Cast:
READER 1
READER 2
READER 3
SCRIPTURE READER
TEMPLE GUARDS
JETHRO
ABNER

Costumes *(optional):*
Readers: choir robes; Temple guards: long-sleeved, turtlenecked shirts and blue jeans

Scenery:
No scenery required

(Hymn)

SCRIPTURE READER: John 7:2 and 37-46

READER 1: As the public ministry of Jesus moved into the last half of the third year, the people's interest in Him rose to fever pitch.

READER 2: The anger and opposition of the Pharisees rose also.

READER 3: One thing that upset them was that Jesus did not give attention to their many rules for observing the Sabbath Day. Jesus always put the needs of people first.

READER 1: They also hated that Jesus was always in control of every situation. No matter how hard they tried to trap Him in His words, or to debate a point of law with Him, Jesus always won. The Pharisees came out second best every time, and it made them look like fools.

READER 2: So they decided to arrest Him. They picked a time when He was in Jerusalem for the Feast of Tabernacles, which would have been in September. Jesus had disrupted things once too often. He had made use of the ceremonial water prayer to give His own message to the people, and both priests and Pharisees were furious.

READER 3: So Temple guards were sent to arrest Jesus. It is important to remember that Temple guards were not necessarily religious men. They were chosen for their physical stature and strength—something like the guards on a football team.

READER 1: But the guards couldn't handle the assignment. The seventh chapter of John's Gospel tells the story. They came back without Jesus.

12

READER 2: Let's listen to an imagined conversation between two Temple guards immediately after their failure to arrest Jesus. We'll call the men Jethro and Abner.

JETHRO: Well, you certainly blew that! Here we are, Temple officers sent by the authorities to arrest this Man, Jesus, and now we've turned up empty-handed.

ABNER: Go on back and finish the job, if you're so keen on it.

JETHRO: It's the first time I was ever sent to arrest a man, and came back without him.

ABNER: Go ahead and arrest Him! He's just one man, and He isn't armed. What's stopping you?

JETHRO: We're supposed to do it together. I'm not anxious to face that mob of Jews alone.

ABNER: I'm not going to do it. They'll just have to send somebody else. When we showed up at the edge of the crowd, and started toward Him—do you remember?—He just turned and looked at us. Never said a word to us, never raised His hand, but it was like a command to halt. I just froze in my tracks. He's not just some ordinary guy, this Jesus. There's power in Him.

JETHRO: There's power in those Pharisees too! What kind of story are we supposed to give them? That He looked at us, and we quit cold?

ABNER: I'm not trying to tell you what to do. I'm just telling you about me. I'm not going to arrest Jesus of Nazareth. He has more authority in His little finger than all that bunch of Temple priests put together. Haven't you heard what the crowd's have been saying about Him? Didn't you just hear what He was saying about himself? I never heard anybody talk like that in my whole life. Suppose it's true—that He is the Christ, the Messiah. Do you want Him remembering you as some-body who tried to arrest Him, like a common criminal? I wouldn't lay hands on Him for a thousand gold pieces!

JETHRO: He certainly made a stir, didn't He? Remember when He stood up, right in the middle of the service? The priest was getting ready to offer the prayer for water, and Jesus suddenly called out, "If anyone thirst, let him come to me and drink!" I tell you, I thought that old priest would drop his water pot on the altar!

ABNER: He could have started a riot a dozen times, but He didn't. The Pharisees have been mad enough to kill Him ever since He healed that cripple at the Bethesda pool on the Sabbath. Did you know that guy? I did! His legs had been paralyzed and withered for 38 years—and now he's as sound as I am, up walking around. If Jesus has the power to raise a man like that, maybe He's got the power to strike him down too!

13

JETHRO: Well, I see your point. But I think we're laying our jobs on the line. What are we going to say?

ABNER: I can't see saying anything but the truth—that nobody ever talked like this Man before, or acted like Him, either.

JETHRO: OK. I guess that's all we've got. But they aren't going to like it. I sure would like to know what's going to happen.

The Centurion at the Cross

by Cynthia S. Baker

Cast:
> READER A
> READER B
> READER C
> READER D
> VOICE 1
> VOICE 2
> VOICE 3
> CORNELIUS: the centurion at the Cross
> MARCUS: a fellow centurion

Costumes and scenery:
This play can be performed effectively with a minimum of preparation as a chancel drama—the parts rehearsed, but read rather than memorized. No scenery, no costumes. Or it can be done as elaborately as anyone wishes.

Scripture references: Matthew 27:27-54; Luke 23:1-49

(Hymn)

READER A: At the crucifixion of our Lord Jesus, one of the people who played an important part was the Roman centurion, the Roman officer in charge of the execution. We wish we knew more about him. The Gospels give us only a glimpse of him, but it is an astonishing glimpse.

READER B: Imagine the scene. Our wonderful, gentle Lord had been cruelly nailed to a rough, wooden cross that was planted upright in the ground so that people could watch Him die. There was a noisy mob of people, all kinds of people, milling around.

READER C: The wicked Temple priests were there. They were responsible for His death, and they were taunting Him.

VOICE 1: Let the Christ, the King of Israel, come down from the Cross, that we may see, and believe!

VOICE 2: Aha! You who would destroy the Temple, and build it in three days, save yourself and come down from the Cross!

VOICE 3: He saved others; let Him save himself if He is the Christ, the chosen one of God!

READER A: Even one of the thieves, crucified beside Him, joined in.

VOICE 4: If You are the Christ, save yourself, and us.

READER B: In the background, the women were wailing and weeping.

15

READER C: The frightened disciples of Jesus were trying to hide themselves in the crowd for fear of arrest.

READER A: The soldiers who had had to do the dreadful job were gambling with dice for Jesus' robe, which was woven without a seam.

READER B: But the Bible tells us that, in the midst of all this, the Roman officer in charge of the execution squad was looking up at the dying Jesus and saying,

CORNELIUS: Truly, this man was the Son of God!

READER C: This officer was a Roman. Romans didn't worship the true God; they worshiped the many Roman gods and goddesses, if they worshiped at all.

READER A: This officer was a centurion, meaning "captain of a hundred men." He was a soldier in the Roman army, which was known for its harsh discipline and its cruelty to enemies.

READER B: You would not have expected such a man to be kind or good. He did, after all, follow Governor Pilate's instructions and order his soldiers to crucify Jesus.

READER C: But from his one recorded statement, we believe that he must have known who Jesus was. Let us listen in on a conversation that might have taken place that evening, between the centurion, Cornelius, and a fellow officer named Marcus, who had not been present at Jesus' crucifixion.

MARCUS: Cornelius, you must pull yourself together! I don't know what on earth happened today to shake you up like this, but it isn't good for the soldiers to see. You're a Roman centurion—try to remember it!

CORNELIUS: Shall I tell *you* something? After today, I don't think that's anything to be proud of!

MARCUS: Lower your voice! Someone will hear you—the walls have ears! Here, man, sit down, have a glass of wine, and compose yourself. You'd better tell me about it. Maybe that will make you feel better.

CORNELIUS *(bitterly):* I don't think I'll ever feel better again. Do you know what I saw today, Marcus? I saw Pilate, the mighty governor of the mighty Roman empire, cowed into submission by a pack of bloodthirsty Jews. I saw Pilate condemn a man whom he knew to be innocent, to public scourging, and ridicule, and to the cruelest kind of death we know, because Pilate didn't have the courage to do what he knew was right. I saw a whole battalion of brave Roman soldiers torturing a kind and noble man who couldn't defend himself.

MARCUS: Wait a minute, wait a minute—He must have done *something* wrong! Why would the Jews have brought Him to Pilate, if He wasn't guilty?

CORNELIUS: Oh sure! That's what *they* said too! What kind of a reason is that? You know as well as I do, there are dozens of reasons why a decent, good man can be accused by his enemies! In fact, in the kind of world this is getting to be, I'd say the good man doesn't stand a chance. When Pilate asked the mob who they wanted him to release, in accordance with the Passover custom of releasing one prisoner, do you know who they asked for? Barabbas, that's who! Barabbas, the robber and murderer! They wanted *him* to go free. And they wanted *Jesus* to be crucified!

MARCUS: Try to calm down, Cornelius! After all, it wasn't your doing.

CORNELIUS: Oh, wasn't it? That isn't even the worst part. So we led Jesus out of the city, to be crucified. He had been severely scourged, and was bleeding so badly it was all He could do to stay on His feet. We had to compel one of the bystanders to carry the Cross for Him. And we nailed Him up on the Cross, with a couple of thieves on both sides— and they were spitting out curses on us, but not an evil word came from Jesus. He looked down from that cross, Marcus, right at me, and said, "Father, forgive them, for they know not what they do." I could have wept.

MARCUS: You keep calling him by name. Did you know the man?

CORNELIUS: I knew what He was like. I heard Him talk more than once. He never did a bad thing, or said a bad word. He healed people, and taught people, and He is said to have done miracles, although I wouldn't know about that.

MARCUS: What was the charge against Him?

CORNELIUS: Blasphemy.

MARCUS: *Blasphemy!* You've got to be kidding! That would be Jewish business, not Roman!

CORNELIUS: You know that, and I know that. But that was the charge. That was why He died. Pilate wrote on the marker over His head, "King of the Jews," in three languages.

MARCUS: Did this Jesus claim to be some kind of god?

CORNELIUS: Not *a* god. He said he was the Son of God—*the* God. Jews only believe in one God. And you know something, Marcus? If ever a man was the Son of God, this Jesus was that man. There's something else too. He called himself "the Light of the World." Do you remember what happened today, around three?

MARCUS: You mean that strange darkness, and the earthquake?

CORNELIUS: That's what I mean.

MARCUS: But surely you don't think there's any connection!

17

CORNELIUS: Yes, I do. I believe it got dark because we had killed the Light of the World. And I believe the ground was shaking with anger of His Father, the one God. I'm still shaking myself. I would give everything I have if I had never had any part in it.

MARCUS: You'd better keep that to yourself, Cornelius. After all, you've seen the last of this Jesus now.

CORNELIUS: I wouldn't bet on it. Even now, even after one of the soldiers thrust a spear right through His heart, I'm not at all sure we've heard the last of Him. If His Father really *is* God—then who knows?

(Hymn)

The Story of the Cross

An Easter Drama Using Slides and Easy-to-Find Musical Selections

by Elaine Cunningham

Scene: Spotlight a cross throughout or use a slide of a cross at the beginning and end of slide presentations. Use other slides as listed. If you do not have a set of slides of the life of Christ, take slide photos of appropriate pictures in books or magazines.

Cast:
NARRATOR
FIRST BOY
SECOND BOY
FIRST MAN
SECOND MAN
CHILD'S VOICE
MOTHER'S VOICE
FIRST WOMAN
SECOND WOMAN
MALE VOICE
MARY

(Readers may use a microphone behind a screen or in a room adjoining the platform. Another option would be to record the voices on cassette tape.)

NARRATOR: I am the Cross. My story is thrilling. Even after nearly 2,000 years, I can't get over the wonder of it.

(A soloist sings verse 2 and chorus of "The Old Rugged Cross." Note: Hymns used will be found in most hymnals.)

NARRATOR: I was a tree growing on a hillside overlooking Jerusalem when I first heard the name of Jesus. Two children ran past me through the woods. Not many people came into my forest, so I listened carefully to what they were saying . . .

FIRST BOY: Am I ever glad we found this shortcut through the woods. We'll get there in time to see Jesus enter the city.

19

SECOND BOY: You know, I really believe He will be our King. Do you suppose He will be in a chariot with white horses pulling it?

FIRST BOY: I don't know, but it's going to be exciting, and we'd better hurry or we'll miss it!

SECOND BOY: Grab some branches from one of those trees so we can put them in the road when He goes by us.

(Project slide of the triumphal entry.)

NARRATOR: Later I heard He didn't ride in a chariot but only on a humble little donkey. But as He rode through the city the people shouted, "Hosanna," and "Crown Him King!"

(Choir sings verse 1 and chorus of "Crown Him.")

NARRATOR: The next time I heard of Jesus I saw Him myself. He and 11 men walked slowly past me at night on their way to the Garden of Gethsemane. He left 8 of the men at the edge of the garden and took 3 of them farther in. I heard Him ask then to wait and watch. Then He went on into the garden—alone.

(Project slide of Jesus praying in Gethsemane. Solo, duet, or trio sings three verses of "Alone." Project slide of betrayal and arrest.)

NARRATOR: Soon I heard men's voices—loud and angry.

FIRST MAN: Get out of the way.

SECOND MAN: There He is.

FIRST MAN: Grab Him!

NARRATOR: Torches were flickering here and there in the darkness. I saw the glint of steel as light shone on swords and helmets. The whole scene puzzled me. A man went up to Jesus and kissed Him, right in the middle of the mob. Other men grabbed Jesus, and they marched down the hill holding Him prisoner.

(Soloist [with choir on chorus] sings verses 1 and 2 of "Ten Thousand Angels." Project slide of Jesus beaten and mocked during song.)

NARRATOR: The next I knew, men ran toward me in the woods. They struck me with their axes. I tried to cry out, "What are you doing to me? Where are you taking me?" But the only sound was a mighty groan and then a crash as I hit the ground. They slashed off my outer bark and dragged me toward the city. During that rough, jolting trip, my entire life flashed before me. I remembered as a child I asked . . .

CHILD'S VOICE: Mother, what will I do when I'm grown up? Do you suppose I will be made into a ship or something great?

MOTHER'S VOICE: What would you like to be, my child?

CHILD'S VOICE: Well, Mother, I really don't want to leave the forest. I'd rather stay here and point people to God. I've heard them say how tall and straight I am. If I grow strong and beautiful, I will remind them of the mighty Creator of us all.

MOTHER'S VOICE: That is a very worthy wish, my child. What better thing could you do in life than to point people to God?

NARRATOR: Now they roughly dragged me out of the forest. My heart broke. As we neared the city other men came and sawed two huge planks from my trunk. They nailed them together with spikes. I looked down at my shape and could not believe what I saw. I was a cross! Criminals died on crosses. To think that I, who wanted to point people to God, would be used as an instrument of death for a thief or murderer. My shame was more than I could bear. The men dragged me down the street toward the criminal who was to die. As we came closer, I looked in horror. Jesus was pushed toward me.

(Project slide of the journey to Golgotha.)

NARRATOR: His kind eyes blurred with pain. His bleeding back and head drooped in agony. I tried to make myself lighter as they slammed me upon His back. Even with my efforts to help, He walked only a few steps, stumbled, and fell. How can they do this to Him? Can't they see He is innocent? How I wished for a voice to cry out against this injustice. But worse was to come . . .

(Soloist or choir sings verses 1, 2, and 3 of "Were You There?" Project slide of the Crucifixion during the song.)

NARRATOR: As I trembled under the burden of the awful scene I heard a soldier say, "Truly this man was the Son of God." Somehow I began to understand. I really was part of a miracle! All my life I wanted to point people to God, and now I held the Son of God on my outstretched arms. I began to see how I would become a symbol of salvation . . . the Cross of Calvary where the Son of God died for the sins of the world.

(Project slide of Jesus on the Cross. Men in unison sing verse 3 of "How Great Thou Art." Choir joins in on chorus.)

NARRATOR: The sky grew dark, lightning flashed, thunder rumbled. People ran in fear. Jesus and I, with a thief on either side, waited alone. I knew He was dead, and the terror of it overwhelmed me. Two men came and removed His body. I heard them say they would bury Him in the tomb of Joseph of Arimathea. After they left it was deathly still on Mount Calvary.

(Project slide of the burial of Jesus.)

NARRATOR: For two days I stood on that windy place of the skull. Early in the morning of the third day, I looked down and saw three women hurrying along the road that went past the foot of the hill. The wind carried their voices up to me . . .

FIRST WOMAN: I just thought of something, Mary. How will we remove the stone from the tomb so we can anoint His body?

SECOND WOMAN: I was thinking of that too. But I feel in my heart we should go. God will guide us. It is the least we can do for the Master.

NARRATOR: They went into the garden of Joseph and approached the sepulchre. Suddenly they stopped!

(Project slide of resurrection morning.)

NARRATOR: Two bright shinging angels spoke to them. The stone was gone from the entrance. The sepulchre was empty!

(Choir sings all verses of "Christ Arose" beginning with chorus. Project slide of Jesus appearing to Mary.)

NARRATOR: Two of the women ran toward the city. After they left, the third woman waited in the garden. She was weeping. A man came toward her and asked . . .

MALE VOICE: Woman, why are you crying? Who are you looking for?

MARY: Sir, if you have carried Him away, tell me where you have put Him.

NARRATOR: He spoke one word only.

MALE VOICE: Mary!

NARRATOR: She looked up. It was Jesus! Her Master and Lord was alive!

(Ladies' duet or choir sings all verses of "I Know That My Redeemer Liveth.")

NARRATOR: Yes, it was Jesus. How thrilled I was when I heard the news. I knew He was alive. My shame vanished. He was alive. He is alive, forevermore!

(Choir sings all verses of "He Lives." Spotlight back on cross or project slide of cross again.)

NARRATOR: Yes, that is my story. I, the little tree who wanted to stay in the forest and point people to God, took part in a miracle . . . the miracle of redemption. Jesus Christ died that all might live. Through believing in Him all mankind could be saved. He is the Savior, Redeemer, and King of Kings. Hallelujah!

(Choir sings all verses of "Hallelujah for the Cross." Light fades out on cross or gradually darken slide of cross.)

The Road

A Play for Easter Evening

by Richard Turpen

Scenes:

Scene 1
Time: A morning three days after the Crucifixion
Place: A road leading from Jerusalem to Emmaus

Scene 2
Time: 70 years prior to crucifixion of Jesus
Place: Simeon's room

Scene 3
Time and place same as scene 1

Scene 4
Time: Eight days following the birth of Jesus
Place: Street scene in Jerusalem

Scene 5
Time: Immediately following scene 4
Place: Interior of the Temple in Jerusalem

Scene 6
Time and place same as scene 1

Cast (In order of appearance):
CLEOPAS
JOSEPH
STRANGER
SIMEON
DAVID
PROPHET
VOICE 1
TEACHER
VOICE 2
EPICUREAN
VOICE 3
FOLLOWER 1
FOLLOWER 2
LEADER: a false prophet
JOSEPH: Mary's husband
MARY

Scene 1

(The curtain rises on a section of a rocky wilderness road. Huge boulders almost waist high dominate the stage. They hide a view of the path that runs

23

from ground level behind them, up across the stage, then down again to ground level in front of the rocks. It is late morning. CLEOPAS *trudges the upward path slowly and pauses for a moment at the top before the second part of the path leading downward. He looks offstage in the direction from which he has come.)*

CLEOPAS: Hurry, Joseph! *(Looks searchingly in the same direction)* I don't see anyone behind us.

*(*JOSEPH *appears and begins the same ascent in the same tired manner.)*

CLEOPAS: Perhaps no one cares. We may be fleeing from nothing.

JOSEPH: We could have stayed in the city and soon found out, Cleopas.

CLEOPAS *(ignores the sarcasm):* When we came from the Passover last week, I never thought we'd have to crawl away before it ended.

JOSEPH: Not after the welcome we got. Just seven days ago and all Jerusalem was at our feet . . . and for the last two we've been afraid someone would recognize us. These hills and rocks are worse than the plague! How much farther is it to Emmaus?

CLEOPAS: About 40 furlongs, I think. *(Starts down the path)* We've barely come half the—OHH!

(He suddenly turns ankle on a rock and falls to the ground in pain.)

JOSEPH: Cleopas! Are you hurt? What is it? Can I help you?

CLEOPAS *(short of breath):* My ankle. *(Clutching it)* Be all right.

JOSEPH: Can you stand up? Let me help you.

(Helps him down remainder of path to level ground where CLEOPAS *can be seated on a rock.* JOSEPH *kneels to examine the injury.)*

JOSEPH: It's beginning to swell already. What are we going to do?

CLEOPAS: Is anyone coming?

*(*JOSEPH *goes to top and looks closely behind them, then returns.)*

JOSEPH: No one in sight, Cleopas.

CLEOPAS: Good. Give me a few minutes. We'll be all right. Needed the rest anyway.

JOSEPH: Of all the luck! Will nothing ever go right again?

CLEOPAS: They haven't caught us yet, Joseph . . . and they've come closer than this. Remember how we slept the night they took Jesus by surprise?

JOSEPH: Yes . . . and there was that man hiding when we were watching them put His body in the cave.

24

CLEOPAS *(bitter):* Unanointed. No time even for a decent burial. They break their own laws to kill a lawbreaker!

JOSEPH: And now, perhaps, they follow His followers!

CLEOPAS: This is no time for humor.

JOSEPH: At least now we can take the time to eat. I've hardly had a thing for three days. Where is our bread?

CLEOPAS: The bread? Don't you have it, Joseph?

JOSEPH: No! Oh no! Don't tell me you forgot to bring food?

CLEOPAS: I thought you did. Well, there's nothing to be done about it now.

JOSEPH *(mimicking):* Oh, there's nothing to be done about it now? How can you be so stupid?

CLEOPAS: Oh, stop it, Joseph. It won't be the first time we've gone hungry. When we were with the Master, no one knew where our next meal was coming from.

JOSEPH: But that was for a cause! At least, I thought so at the time.

CLEOPAS: Control yourself, man. You haven't been the same since He was taken.

JOSEPH: And why shouldn't that change me? Do you think I like to play the fool?

CLEOPAS: What do you mean? What makes you a fool?

JOSEPH: You must be blind, Cleopas. Don't you see how we were deceived? I thought you must surely have realized it by now.

(A robed figure appears behind the rocks. He stands motionless, watching the men argue.)

CLEOPAS: I don't know what you're talking about. Do you feel foolish because we're fleeing from the Romans and the priests? I don't see anything foolish about evading crucifixion.

JOSEPH: Exactly! Yet Jesus didn't avoid it! He goaded the priests every day—almost on purpose it seemed—and then refused to defend himself when they lost patience. He practically committed suicide because of His poor judgment! And where is our hope for a free Israel now?

CLEOPAS: What does that matter? His perspective was greater than that. Jesus was bringing more than freedom for our land. He would have taught us all a new way of life . . . a way of love.

JOSEPH: That's beside the point. Certainly He was a good, virtuos man, but He was a fool too! He had most of the people with us and then made the mistake of antagonizing their leaders. He made His direct attack too quickly—too soon.

CLEOPAS: Attack? Jesus never had anything to do with "attack." You never saw His true aims at all. *(Suddenly a shade of bitterness)* If God had not deserted Him in the hour of crisis, He might have shown men how to live . . .

JOSEPH: Under the Romans? That's not living! No, freedom for His people—that was His real aim. Only He understood the power of our priests, who get their power from Rome and fear that a revolution would cause them to be suppressed too.

CLEOPAS: If God had remained with Him, no power on earth could have forced Him to the miserable end He saw, and if your eyes were not completely blinded by politics, Joseph, you must surely have seen that God was with Him when we knew Him. *(To himself)* So why was He left to die on the Cross? What wrong did He do?

JOSEPH: I told you! I've told you again and again, but you seem to see Him in some sentimental haze—as if He wished only to coax everyone to be loving and kind. He was a man of action, I tell you!

CLEOPAS: And His actions have brought us to this. *(Clutches ankle)* Oh! Is there anyone behind us, Joseph? Look down the road.

JOSEPH: Just a minute.

(Ascends path to top, stops and looks intensely off. He is staring right through the STRANGER. *The* STRANGER *is apparently invisible to both.* JOSEPH *returns.)*

JOSEPH: Some luck is still with us. There's not a soul in sight. How's your leg?

(They have both cooled off by now. CLEOPAS *attempts to stand but sinks back under his weight.)*

CLEOPAS: No better, but we cannot stay here. What are we going to do, Joseph? There's no telling what persecutions await the followers of a convicted blasphemer.

JOSEPH: . . . and revolutionist. From the tales we heard, they were not easy on Him. Have you ever seen a crucifixion, Cleopas?

CLEOPAS *(shudders)*: Once, when I was a boy. I could never stand it! I'd take my own life first. Yes, suicide would be far better than what they have waiting for us back there. *(Gestures)* I wonder where the others are now?

CLEOPAS: Running away, too, I suppose. I pray they're all away from the city anyway. Jesus seemed to be holding us together . . . when He was taken everyone disappeared so quickly! Strange, isn't it? Many authorities were angry with us when we were with Him—yet we never felt fear.

JOSEPH: We never expected their measures to be so drastic, either.

(CLEOPAS *continues on his own train of thought.*)

CLEOPAS: It must have been our faith . . . the trust we had in His every action.

JOSEPH: The trust He betrayed with His overconfidence. I tell you, Cleopas, the power He had over people gave Him a duty to His country.

(The STRANGER *in the background moves for the first time. He begins walking up the path.)*

CLEOPAS: What was that? Did you hear?

JOSEPH: Someone's coming! What shall we do?

CLEOPAS: What CAN we do? I cannot move. Perhaps we can get help.

JOSEPH: Look! It's only one man. We've nothing to fear—and maybe he has food.

(The STRANGER *has reached the top of the path.)*

JOSEPH: The blessings of the Lord be upon you, traveler.

STRANGER: Peace be unto you, my friends. This is a hard road, is it not?

JOSEPH: Indeed yes. My friend here has been hurt, and we thought you might be good enough to help us on our way. You're bound for Emmaus, too, I take it?

(The STRANGER *moves beside* CLEOPAS.*)*

STRANGER: Perhaps I can help you.

CLEOPAS: It's my ankle. I stumbled, but it will be all right in time.

STRANGER: Yes, time is a good healer, but not the only one. Let me see you stand and walk.

CLEOPAS: But . . .

(The STRANGER *takes his hand and* CLEOPAS *rises in bewilderment, then in amazement as his pain disappears.)*

CLEOPAS: Joseph! I can walk on it!

JOSEPH: There's no pain?

CLEOPAS: None at all! *(To the* STRANGER) It's amazing! How did you do it? Are you a holy man?

STRANGER *(smiles):* Have you ever seen a holy man without followers?

CLEOPAS: However you did it, I'm grateful to you. *(He walks about experimentally.)*

JOSEPH: We both are.

STRANGER: You say you are traveling to Emmaus. It must be very urgent to take you from the city in the midst of Passover.

JOSEPH: Yes, it's urgent, all right. In fact, we left so quickly we forgot to bring our food.

STRANGER: I have a few crusts of bread. You're welcome to share with me.

(The STRANGER and JOSEPH sit on the rocks. CLEOPAS still stands.)

CLEOPAS: You're very kind. Tell me, stranger, has the excitement in the city died down yet?

STRANGER: Oh, no. As I said, the Passover will continue for some time.

JOSEPH *(impatient, yet cautious):* No, no, Cleopas means we understand there was an execution just about the time it began. A man from Nazareth.

STRANGER: Let's see. I believe there were three of them at once.

CLEOPAS: That's it! One of them was named Jesus.

STRANGER: Well, what about Him?

CLEOPAS: We know there will be no more executions during the feast, but we wondered if the Romans or the priests were searching for His followers.

STRANGER: A criminal with followers?

CLEOPAS: Criminal!

STRANGER: Was He not? Then why was He put to death?

CLEOPAS: Why, it was an illegal trick to . . .

JOSEPH: Cleopas! You see, stranger, there was some question about the legality of the trial—and even the charge—but the chief priests undoubtedly did the right thing.

STRANGER: What was the charge?

CLEOPAS: The Jews said blasphemy—the Romans, treason.

STRANGER: And what do you say?

JOSEPH: What do you mean? We were not His judges. You ask more questions than we have answers. We hardly knew the Man.

STRANGER: But you did know Him?

JOSEPH: I think we've talked long enough. Thank you for your help. We're very grateful. *(To* CLEOPAS*)* Come, let's be on our way.

STRANGER: Wait. We haven't eaten yet. Let's rest a moment more. You know, from your questions, I would guess that you two were among this Nazarene's followers.

CLEOPAS: We didn't say that!

STRANGER: But you're not very practiced at hiding your true feelings as many men are.

JOSEPH *(slightly menacing):* You're a good guesser. What are you going to do about it?

STRANGER: Why, nothing. How does it concern me? I'm only interested in the stories all men have to tell—if they would. Tell me, was this Jesus your teacher . . . a holy man, perhaps?

CLEOPAS: I won't lie to you, friend. We thought He was.

JOSEPH: Till we learned better!

STRANGER: And why do you doubt it now? Because of His death? Do not even holy men die?

JOSEPH: Do they fail shamefully in their missions?

CLEOPAS: Joseph! *(To the* STRANGER*)* We differ in our judgments of our teacher, as you can see. He is angry with himself for failing to see certain weaknesses in our rabbi's character . . . while I feel that the blame for the failure belongs to God, not Jesus.

STRANGER: God's failure! That's a strong judgment. You must be mistaken. The Lord works in strange ways, you know.

CLEOPAS: If only you had known Jesus. Then you would understand my feelings. Never was there such a man!

JOSEPH: Still His error was a man's, stranger. He simply miscalculated His powers and went too far.

STRANGER: There's little belief left between you two. You've lost your faith in men and in God. What else is there to stand by you?

JOSEPH: We'll stand alone!

CLEOPAS: Only now, more alone than ever!

STRANGER: Don't desert your beliefs so easily. I told you I was interested in stories. There's one my mother used to tell me about a man who talked with the Lord. His faith was tried to the limit . . . but he didn't give it up.

JOSEPH: We've all heard such stories. It's as well they're told to children—who find them so easy to believe.

STRANGER: Perhaps men would be better off if they were more like children.

CLEOPAS: What do you mean?

STRANGER: Joseph has just told us. Children believe.

CLEOPAS: So did we!

JOSEPH: And now look at us!

STRANGER: Yes, I see.

(JOSEPH *does not like the tone of this last remark.*)

STRANGER: Where have your doubts brought you? There's nothing left of all you had a few short days ago.

JOSEPH: Listen! We didn't ask to be deceived. We're not dodging priests and Romans for our pleasure. We're in this position because we did believe . . . and now I say faith is for fools!

CLEOPAS: Joseph is right, friend. If God would not support that man in His hour of need . . . He must be unaware of our existence.

STRANGER: This man my mother described . . .

JOSEPH: This is no time for stories! For all we know . . .

(JOSEPH *looks toward the city.*)

CLEOPAS: Wait, Joseph! If it had not been for him, we'd still be stranded here. Let him speak.

JOSEPH: But Cleopas, now that . . .

STRANGER: Besides, you haven't eaten yet. *(His most convincing argument)* Let me tell you my story. It will not take much time . . . and then we'll eat.

(JOSEPH *sits down impatiently.*)

JOSEPH: All right. Begin it then. Let's hear about this man whose faith was so much better than ours.

STRANGER: Be not anxious, Joseph. It's not only that the man had faith—but he learned something about the ways of the Lord. I believe it will help you. For one thing, this man—whose name was Simeon—knew that there was a purpose to his life. Didn't you feel the same when you followed the Nazarene?

CLEOPAS: Of course, but now we know . . .

STRANGER: Now you know nothing, because you have let the ground of your belief sink from under you. But let me start at the beginning.

(As the STRANGER *speaks, the lights slowly fade to darkness.)*

STRANGER: It was not a very long time ago. Just as in our day, many looked for the coming of the Messiah—the Lord's Anointed One, who would drive out the foreign rulers and deliver our people to freedom. Simeon was one of these, and he must have been a particularly good and just man or he would never have had this remarkable experience . . .

Scene 2

(The lights on the second set, the interior of SIMEON's *room, become just bright enough to barely make out the man who is on his knees in prayer. The only furnishings are a table and chair. Distant music is heard for about 10 seconds. When it begins,* SIMEON's *head starts upward then drops again when it ceases.*

*(*DAVID *enters the room, straining to see in the dim light. He gropes about the room.)*

DAVID *(questioning tone, not loud):* Simeon, Simeon, are you here? (DAVID *stumbles over the entranced* SIMEON.) Simeon! What are you doing in this darkness? You need light here. Are you praying again? Here, let's get some light into this room.

*(*DAVID *crosses and throws open the door. Light streams in upon the two figures from this source only.* SIMEON, *still dazed and dumb, shakes his head as he returns to his senses.)*

SIMEON: David? Is that you, David? *(Arises)*

DAVID: What did you expect—an angel or something? Really, Simeon, you spend so much time on these "meditations" and prayers that . . .

*(*SIMEON *speaks excitedly, as much to himself as to* DAVID.)*

SIMEON: It did happen, it did! I had a vision, David! A message from the Lord. I can't believe it!

DAVID: What? Well, neither can I, but you might as well tell me about it— you will anyway.

*(*SIMEON *continues, too absorbed to notice* DAVID's *sarcasm.)*

SIMEON: Yes! Yes! He promised me the Christ would come, and soon—in our lifetime!

DAVID: Who promised?

SIMEON: Who? What do you mean, who? *(Patiently explaining)* The spirit of the Lord told me that I would live to see His Messiah—with my own eyes! Don't you understand? This means our people will soon be free again!

31

DAVID *(calm):* Well, this is good news, Simeon. Wonderful news—if it's true.

SIMEON *(shocked):* Would you doubt the word of God, David? His own promise?

DAVID: Of course not. But you see, I haven't heard the word of God. I hear only you, Simeon—and louder than ever before.

SIMEON: You don't believe me. Not a word I've said.

DAVID: How can I, Simeon? I must admit that if God were to speak to any of my friends, it would be you . . . you spend so much time talking to Him. But such things don't happen! You must have fallen asleep at your prayers and dreamed it all.

SIMEON *(to himself again):* Not a word . . . but I would probably doubt it myself if it had been someone else. Though I'm sure it happened! He said, "Simeon—thy faith has supported thee. Thou shalt not see death before thine eyes have seen the Christ." He did!

DAVID: We have always been good friends, Simeon. But you dwell too much on these matters. A little religion goes a long way. Now why don't you just get your mind off the whole thing? Come, join me. You need company, conversation, laughter!

SIMEON: Good company . . . conversation . . . David, don't you see? I have spoken with God!

DAVID *(exasperated):* You're helpless. Look here. Even supposing your story is true, what do you propose to do about it?

SIMEON *(taken aback):* What do you mean?

DAVID: You say you were told you would see the Messiah yourself. Well, what are you going to do? Wait for Him to walk in the front door here? And if He did, how would you know Him? *(Pauses)* Haven't you thought of that?

SIMEON: I've thought of nothing. How could I? It just happened. You're right, though. This matter needs some thought.

DAVID *(pressing his advantage):* Yes, and did your vision tell you where to begin. What to look for? How to recognize the Messiah?

SIMEON: No, no, but it is not for me to question. I have received the word. Now it seems to me I should do something to earn this privilege. Perhaps the Man doesn't even know His real identity . . . perhaps it is part of my task to reveal His mission to Him! For now, it's enough that I have God's word.

DAVID: Well, I came here to invite you to join us at my father's inn. All our friends are there now. Will you come?

SIMEON: No, David. Thank you.

DAVID: They'll enjoy hearing about your experience—a lively discussion.

SIMEON *(losing patience):* Go on! Go to your inn. Have a fine time telling them all how Simeon lost his mind! Leave me alone!

DAVID *(unfazed):* Of course. And later perhaps I can spare the time to go Messiah-hunting with you. *(Pauses at the door, repressing a smile)* Come join us later, if you like.

SIMEON *(staring after him):* The fool!

(SIMEON *walks about restlessly as if hunting for something. He stops and drops to his knees as he did at the opening of the scene. As he prays, the light fades to darkness.)*

Scene 3

(As the STRANGER *talks, lights rise to brightness on the road scene.)*

STRANGER: And so Simeon found himself high in favor with his God. Chosen for what he considered to be a great task, but uncertain as to how to perform it.

JOSEPH: Men have always been fools when it comes to religous and spiritual matters. Why do you feel it necessary to tell us the details about this man's mistakes? Wasn't it just depressing when your mother told it to you?

STRANGER: You have not heard me out. How do you know whether Simeon was a fool—or that he made any mistakes?

CLEOPAS: Why, Joseph's right, it's only common sense, friend. You say Simeon was told he would see the Messiah. Since He has never appeared, even to this day, the man could never have found Him.

JOSEPH: That's right. And we never heard of this Simeon before. He must have passed out of his misery long ago.

STRANGER: You men are so quick to condemn . . . give up so easily. Simeon had faith in the ways of the Lord, where is yours? Where is YOUR vision?

CLEOPAS: We left it buried behind a rock in Jerusalem.

JOSEPH: Yes. Vision and faith are delicate flowers. They are easily crushed by the facts . . . and trampled upon by death! And that reminds me. We'd better check the road again.

CLEOPAS: I'll go!

(CLEOPAS *runs to the top of the road and looks off.* JOSEPH *watches him anxiously until he returns.)*

STRANGER: Is this fear of pursuit related to the death of your former teacher, the Nazarene?

CLEOPAS: Yes. I wouldn't admit this to anyone else . . . but we really believed for a time that Jesus was actually the Anointed One. The Messiah himself!

STRANGER: You did? On what grounds did you base this belief?

CLEOPAS: Why . . . mostly faith I guess. How can I explain? It was not a matter of thought but of feeling. Isn't that right, Joseph?

JOSEPH: I don't know why he's telling you everything, but he's right. We didn't see eye to eye on just what Jesus was—or would have been—but we did agree that He was unusual . . . a man marked for a special mission.

CLEOPAS: If your mother's story were true, he would still have to be waiting for the Messiah. But go on with it and let us hear. What did he decide he must do?

(As the STRANGER *speaks, the lights slowly dim.)*

STRANGER: After much more prayer, Simeon decided that his first impulse was right. That he must do something—must search for the Messiah. He made it his duty to hear every rabbi, every street preacher, anyone, in or out of the Temple, who claimed to bear a message. Even those who said nothing—the silent ones who passed him in the streets, the revolutionaries gathering in secret bands outside the cities in the wilderness—anyone at all who might hold the secret . . .

(Darkness on both sets. Suddenly a spotlight illuminates only the face of the first prophet. The PROPHET *speaks directly to the audience.)*

PROPHET: Oooooh! Heads will roll, my brethren! Heads will roll in the streets! Blood will rain down from the heavens—and great flashes of lightning shall strike the unbelievers dead!

VOICE 1 *(from audience):* You mean Roman heads, prophet?

PROPHET: Yes, friend! I mean Roman heads . . . but not theirs only! All those, too, of our people who have aided them in their power and rule. They defile our blessed land. The destruction will be gigantic, I tell you! Fire and flood will sweep over them! The earth will break open and swallow them by the hundreds! They shall be slain with their own spears! They'll die . . .

VOICE 1: When, prophet? When, will we see it?

PROPHET: The time has not yet been shown unto me, man. But it will be soon, that I know! Soon they'll be crushed into the dusty ground! Soon they'll be torn to shreds! Not one will survive. All Romans *(fading)* and their friends will be battered . . . *(lights out, voice continues)* pierced . . . drowned . . . burned . . .

34

(Darkness and silence again. Spotlight on the face of the TEACHER.)

TEACHER *(to audience):* And so, good friends, if you learn how to live rightly with one another . . . if you follow these few principles, your reward will be a life of peace and goodwill.

VOICE 2 *(from audience):* How can there be peace while Caesar's men rule our land, teacher? Are we not to rise against them or resist them in any way?

TEACHER: No, My son. Of course not. Of what use would it be? We have not the power nor the will to resist them. It is useless . . . but it's also unimportant. What IS important is the way you live under trial. Time will take care of both the Romans and ourselves. What you cannot change, ignore. Do not allow it to affect your life. It never can, unless you and your own will permit it. God's wisdom has placed you in this particular world as a test. Never let that accidental outer world re-place the inner world *(light out as voice continues),* and you will have learned the greatest lesson of them all.

(A third spotlight breaks open the darkness and lights the face of the EPICUREAN.)

EPICUREAN: Many teachers will lay down the strictest rules of conduct for you, my friends. Some will be very hard to follow—and if you do, what benefit have you? You will know nothing more than before. You will be no better off. For who knows what the morrow will bring?

VOICE 3 *(from audience):* Who cares!

EPICUREAN: Precisely! Spoken like a true disciple. Tomorrow is of no impor-tance whatever. We know not even if it will come or not . . . and if it does, whether we shall be here to greet it. So live for today, I say. Till the fields and tend your sheep, if you must—but no more than neces-sary. All the yield is taken from thee anyway. Dance while you can! Sing and be merry! *(Light out, voice continues)* Let us all retire to Brother Jacob's house for supper. He has generously invited us all.

(Complete darkness prevails as the STRANGER *continues his narration.)*

STRANGER: Season after season, Simeon followed every crowd to every new teacher and prophet . . . approaching them with a heart full of faith and hope, but leaving them behind as each one revealed, through his own words, that he was not the Messiah. He saw many wise men—and more fools—over the years . . . until he grew too old and tired to con-tinue his seemingly fruitless search any longer. He had returned to Je-rusalem occasionally during his quest, but finally he decided to go home for good . . . so weary that he wished for nothing more than to fulfill his mission and depart this life in peace.

35

Scene 4

(Lights brighten slowly to reveal a street in Jerusalem. The curtain back-drop has been parted in the center of this half of the stage to form an entrance to the Temple. Across the empty stage to the Temple door walk the robed figures of a man and a woman. They walk slowly. The man is engrossed in the woman and her burden, which is not clear to the audience.

(SIMEON walks on wearily, deep in thought. He is about to follow the couple through the Temple door when he is stopped short by an offstage cry.)

DAVID: Simeon! Is that you? *(Crosses to SIMEON)* I hardly knew you . . . it's been such a long time. What in the world has happened to you? What do you do with yourself in these days?

SIMEON: Greetings, David. You appear to have prospered. As for myself, I still seek the blessed sight of the Messiah.

DAVID: Not really, Simeon! Are you still at it? I can't believe it!

SIMEON: Belief is a strange thing. Look at the way my life has changed because I believed in a voice I heard only once . . . a long time ago. *(Teasing)* You'll remember that it was your own advice that I seek out the Messiah rather than be content to wait here at home.

DAVID: But I only jested, Simeon! I was amazed when you left so suddenly afterward . . . and by now I assumed that you had forgotten your so-called vision and had settled down somewhere as a decent citizen. You mean that you've actually been chasing that ghost all this time? Surely you've given up now. You've been wasting your life.

SIMEON: My life has been full, David. I've seen people and places and things you would never dream of . . . but now I'm tired of journeys. All I want to do is finish my task and rest . . . rest for good. I don't know. What have I done wrong? Why can't I find Him?

DAVID: It's long past time you gave up the whole fantastic idea. Look at me. While you've been trudging around heathen lands I've been building up the business my father left me. I believe I have the finest inn of the city.

SIMEON: Give up? No, I'm too old to give up the habit of a lifetime. I am too weary to continue traveling about on the heels of every countryside prophet . . . but I still hope to see the Man of God, as I was promised.

(SIMEON walks toward the Temple door.)

DAVID: Wait! Where are you going?

SIMEON: Why, into the Temple here, David. It's always my first stop when I arrive in a city . . . and I've just come home.

DAVID: Oh, let it wait, Simeon. I want to talk to you. Tell me, if you can no longer look for Him in other lands, why don't you just stop everything?

(Crowd noise is heard offstage.)

SIMEON: God will bring the Messiah here to me in Jerusalem. He must. I can't travel anymore. Look! See this group approaching?

DAVID: Yes. What about it?

SIMEON: I know that man. I heard him in Cappadocia . . . or was it Ashkenaz? There were so many.

DAVID: He's not the Christ, eh?

SIMEON: He claims to be favored of God, but in practice, he'd prefer that you worship him rather than the Lord.

FOLLOWER 1: Out of the way here, old men!

FOLLOWER 2: Do you block the path of Israel's savior? Move!

SIMEON: Step over here, David. We must not impede the triumphal progress of this great man.

DAVID: I thought you said he was just another faker.

FOLLOWER 2: I heard you—you blasphemer!

FOLLOWER 1: Strike him down with heavenly fire, Rabbi!

LEADER: No! He . . . and all others like unto him . . . will learn the error of their ways at the great day of reckoning—when Jehovah and I judge them all! *(To* SIMEON *and* DAVID*)* But if you come to our gathering now, you may be taught the truth in a simpler—and less painful—way.

DAVID and SIMEON *(in unison):* No.

LEADER *(as if a command):* To the devil with you then! Let's be on our way!

FOLLOWERS *(as they leave):* You were lucky this time, old men. Watch out! You'll get it yet.

DAVID: Well, you certainly don't need a revelation to see whether or not that man is the Christ.

SIMEON: No, but suppose you knew of Him only by reputation? There are many like that . . . each one with a group of followers.

DAVID: I'm surprised you didn't give up long ago. Men like him would have chilled any fever of mine very quickly. Come, you can tell me more of your experiences.

SIMEON: No, no, I told you I was on my way to the Temple.

DAVID: Just stay with me awhile, and then I will go with you to your prayers.

SIMEON: No, I must go alone.

DAVID: But . . . All right. But I want to hear more of your journeys!

(As DAVID exits, SIMEON stands watching him, then turns and enters the Temple. The lights go out.)

Scene 5

(The lights go up, revealing the couple of the previous scene standing with their backs to the audience. They are facing a lectern, the only furnishing. (SIMEON enters and stops. He speaks to himself as if thinking.)

SIMEON: What a strange feeling. Something seems to be different in this temple. Is it possible that HE could be here now? Teaching or praying . . . right here at home after all that traveling? No, there's only that couple there. They must be waiting to name their child. But I still have that feeling . . . and they're the only ones here. Perhaps I should draw near—my eyes are no longer so young. (Simeon begins to walk across the stage. He stops, stunned.) Oh, my Lord . . . IT IS! The Christ is a child! (SIMEON *approaches the couple.)*

SIMEON: Woman!

JOSEPH: What's this? Are you the rabbi? We're waiting to name this child. Do you perform this ceremony?

SIMEON: No, no. Forgive me, please! But this babe you have. Do you know who He is? Do you know what He means to us?

Joseph: Yes, man, but— Do you know this man, Mary?

(MARY shakes her head.)

JOSEPH: Our child has already seen more than His share of strange things. There were the animals . . . and the shepherds . . . and now, what's this?

SIMEON: Behold! This child will cause the fall . . . and rising again . . . of many in Israel—and a sign that shall be spoken against! The thoughts of many hearts will be revealed . . . *(To* MARY) Yes, and a sword shall pierce through your soul too!

MARY: I don't understand you, old man.

SIMEON: No matter. Tell me, what will you call HIM?

MARY: I was told that His name should be called Jesus.

SIMEON *(savoring the name):* Jesus. Please, may I hold this wondrous child . . . in my own arms? *(Receives the child)* How old is He now?

JOSEPH: He was born eight days ago, old man.

SIMEON *(wonderment):* Eight days. Only eight days on this earth. *(Laughs in exuberance)* For years I searched for a wise old man or a brilliant young teacher . . . and now . . . HERE is the Messiah, a babe in my arms! Who can understand the Lord? Blessed be His name. Here, take Him. My prayers have been answered and my search is ended.

(Lights dim to darkness, except for a faint spotlight on SIMEON's *face as he looks up in prayer.)*

SIMEON: O Lord, now let Your servant depart in peace according to Thy word. For mine eyes have seen Thy salvation, a light to lighten the Gentiles . . . and the glory of Thy people Israel!

(Darkness.)

Scene 6

(Lights brighten on the road scene.)

STRANGER: So at last Simeon's life purpose was fulfilled and he saw the Savior of his people . . .

JOSEPH: Hold, stranger! He saw a CHILD and knew it to be the Messiah? That's hard to believe.

STRANGER: The truth is often so.

CLEOPAS: But the Baby he saw . . . Didn't you say His name was Jesus? Could He . . .

STRANGER: Yes. The same man you called Jesus of Nazareth, Cleopas.

CLEOPAS: No, your story can't be true! It's possible that Simeon saw our Master in the Temple . . . but Simeon was wrong. Jesus can't have been the Christ!

JOSEPH: That's right! We told you Jesus was crucified. We saw His grave! How can the Messiah die without fulfilling His mission? Without BE-ING a Messiah?

STRANGER: That's why I told you about Simeon, that you might understand. All men try to twist God's word to fit their own ideas. Simeon was wrong in his ideas of what the Messiah would BE—you, in what the Messiah would DO!

CLEOPAS: You mean He actually WAS the promised Man of God? He was? I wanted to believe it . . . I do want to, but how can I when He's dead?

STRANGER: O fools and slow of heart to believe the unfolding of the prophets. Ought not Christ to have suffered these things and enter into His glory? Simeon spent his life looking for the Christ. When he finally found the baby Jesus, he saw only the very beginning of that life . . . much more was to come. You worked with Jesus during His ministry—

39

and at His death. Perhaps you see only the beginning of an even greater unfolding . . . with much more to come!

CLEOPAS: Tell us again.

JOSEPH: What does it mean?

STRANGER: But you two haven't eaten yet.

(JOSEPH *moves.*)

STRANGER: Wait! Let me break this bread for you. *(He does so.)* Take this and eat.

(They accept and begin to eat distractedly, their minds full of this mystery. The STRANGER *walks over to one side and stands watching them.* JOSEPH *speaks to* CLEOPAS, *who is deep in his thoughts.)*

JOSEPH: What is He trying to tell us, Cleopas?

CLEOPAS: Joseph! Yes, I know it now. Look! Where did He go?

JOSEPH *(confused):* What? *(Repeats without understanding)* Where did He go?

CLEOPAS: He's gone, Joseph! The traveler's gone! I understand all! The way He cured my injury—the story His mother told Him—and now, when He broke and blessed this bread . . .

JOSEPH: The bread! You mean it was . . . the Master? Here with us?

CLEOPAS: It's the only explanation, Joseph.

JOSEPH: But He was dead. We KNOW He was dead!

CLEOPAS *(going up the path):* That's the meaning of it. He WAS dead—but Jesus now lives!

(Music)

JOSEPH *(when* CLEOPAS *starts down):* Wait! Where are you going? You're going the wrong way . . . you're going back to the city.

CLEOPAS: Yes! Yes, Joseph, back to the city. The RIGHT way, Joseph! Back to Jerusalem. This is only the beginning!

(Curtain.)

Alleluia! Alleluia!

CHRISTOPHER WORDSWORTH

LUDWIG VAN BEETHOVEN
EDWARD HODGES

1. Al - le - lu - ia! Al - le - lu - ia! Hearts to heav'n and voic - es raise.
2. Now the i - ron bars are bro - ken; Christ from death to life is born–
3. Al - le - lu - ia! Al - le - lu - ia! Glo - ry be to God on high.

Sing to God a hymn of glad-ness; Sing to God a hymn of praise.
Glo - rious life, and life im - mor - tal On this res - ur - rec - tion morn.
Al - le - lu - ia to the Sav-ior Who has won the vic - to - ry.

He who on the cross as Sav-ior For the world's sal - va - tion bled,
Christ has tri-umphed, and we con-quer By His might-y en - ter-prise;
Al - le - lu - ia to the Spir- it, Fount of love and sanc-ti - ty.

Je - sus Christ, the King of Glo-ry, Now is ris - en from the dead.
We with Him to life e - ter-nal By His res - ur - rec-tion rise.
Al - le - lu - ia! Al - le - lu - ia To the Tri-une Maj - es-ty.

Jesus Is Lord

ED SEABOUGH   OTIS SKILLINGS

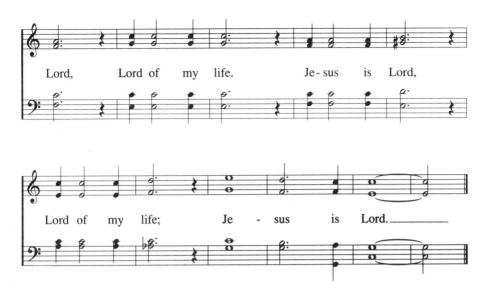

Lord, Lord of my life. Je-sus is Lord,

Lord of my life; Je - sus is Lord.

He Is Lord

Based on Philippians 2:11

Anonymous

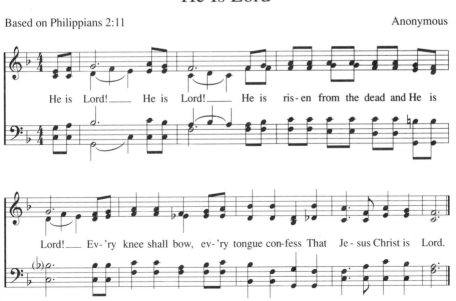

He is Lord!___ He is Lord!___ He is ris-en from the dead and He is

Lord!___ Ev-'ry knee shall bow, ev-'ry tongue con-fess That Je-sus Christ is Lord.

He Is Risen Like He Said

S. P. P.

STEVEN P. PETERSON

With excitement

He is not here; He's ris - en. The gift of life is giv - en. He o - ver - came death's pris - on and He's ris - en from the dead. Dry all the tears of sor - row; We have no grief to bor - row. Now we can face to - mor - row for He's ris - en like He

3rd time to Coda

said.

1. He has cap - tured ev - 'ry fear and
2. Death, O death, where is your sting; where

con - quered ev - 'ry foe.
is your dark do - main?

For

See Him bruise the
you've been ren - dered

1st time: D.C.
2nd time: D.C. al Coda

ser - pent's head with one tri - um - phant blow.
pow - er - less by His vic - to - rious reign.

CODA

said. He's ris - en like He said.

45